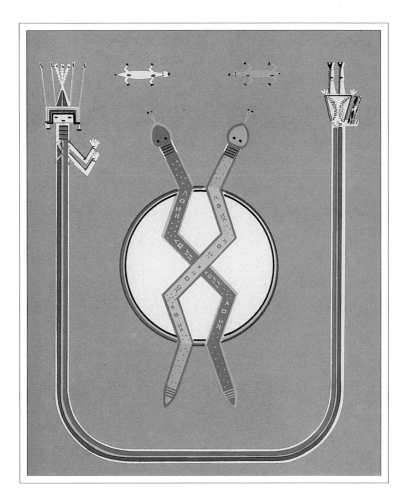

NAVAJO

WALKING IN BEAUTY

NATIVE AMERICAN WISDOM

CHRONICLE BOOKS

SAN FRANCISCO

A Labyrinth Book

First published in the United States in 1994 by Chronicle Books.

Copyright © 1994 by Labyrinth Publishing (UK) Ltd.

Design by Meringue Management

The Little Wisdom Library–Native American Wisdom was produced by Labyrinth Publishing (UK) Ltd. Printed and bound in Singapore by Craft Print Pte. Ltd.

Library of Congress Cataloging-in-Publication Data: Navajo, Native American Wisdom.

p.   cm. (Native American Wisdom) Includes bibliographical references.

ISBN 0–8118–0442–9

1. Navajo Indians—Folklore. 2. Navajo Indians—Social life and customs.

3. Navajo Indians—Philosophy. I. Chronicle Books (Firm) II. Series.

E99. N3N277   1994

979'. 004972—dc20   92–44202
                                                           CIP

Distributed in Canada by Raincoast Books,

112 East Third Avenue, Vancouver, B.C. V5T 1C8

10 9 8 7 6 5 4 3 2 1

Chronicle Books

275 Fifth Street, San Francisco, CA 94103

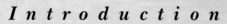

Introduction

T he imposing geography and climate of the American Southwest inspire many visitors to endow those who live there with magical, mystical qualities. Remote from the nation's population centers, and too forbidding a place for many even to consider for permanent settlement, the deserts and mountains with their dry heat evoke awe for the Navajos who maintain the nation's largest reservation in this rough country, yet walk in serene beauty. These desert dwellers have achieved a mastery particular to this universe: tending flocks of sheep and goats, weaving rugs that fetch thousands of dollars at auction, fashioning jewelry of silver and turquoise, dry-painting healing pictures in the sand.

The visitor readily believes that the Navajo Nation must have endured for millennia to achieve such harmony with the land of enchantment. Actually the tribe that now governs not only the Big Reservation but three smaller noncontiguous ones is a relative latecomer to the region, arriving about the time that Columbus set

hunting people. From wherever they came, the newcomers were likely impressed by the cliff dwellings and mesa-top pueblos whose builders raised corn, beans, and squash, wove cotton blankets, turned pots, and stripped veins of coal for fuel. Certainly they pursued this abundance; the Navajos raided the pueblos, mated with the women they stole, and eventually learned and adopted many of the material and spiritual ways of their victims.

The Navajos are Native America's quintessential adapters. This is not to suggest that they borrowed all and contributed

sail for the Spice Islands in 1492. Athabascan speakers, the Navajos are linguistically related to the tribes inhabiting the Canadian Northwest, leading scholars to hypothesize a southerly trek by a

Previous page 4: A sand painting used in healing ceremonials. The rainbow guardian encircling the snake features in the great majority of Navajo sand paintings. *Page 7:* Bolo ornament fashioned of turquoise and silver. *Page 8:* This mountainous terrain now known as the Painted Desert was once part of Navajo territory. *Above:* The figures woven into this blanket depict the Holy People of the Navajo tradition.

nothing; rather, they assimilated the usable to ways of their own. Although they abandoned nomadic wandering and raiding in favor of sheepherding and blanket weaving, the tribespeople eschewed village life, building their conical hogans

harm from powerful entities, ghosts, and witchery. The Navajos recognized the difficulties inherent in following a path of beauty through life, so they devised an intricate system to maintain a precarious balance in the midst of good and evil.

at wide intervals to accommodate their livestock. The Navajos' metaphysical well-being, too, has sprung from the mix of their own traditions and the ancient beliefs of the Pueblo people. The result: a complex, ritualized existence in which constant watchfulness prevents personal and collective

If this largest U.S. tribe views itself today as among the last of the really traditional Indians, the near arrogance can be understood. The Navajos' adaptability has enabled them to thrive in the face of tribulation. Climaxing

Above: Portrait of a Navajo man taken in the 1880s.
Opposite: Portrait of Elle, known as the best weaver of her time, who made a blanket for President Theodore Roosevelt. Hand-tinted postcard of 1906.

an Anglo-American campaign to bring the tribe's raiding activities to an end, Kit Carson led a victorious thrust against the Navajos who had sought a final sanctuary at Canyon de Chelly. Hundreds were captured, imprisoned, and then forced along with others numbering eight thousand on the still-remembered Long Walk of three hundred miles east, to a New Mexico reservation, in 1864. Years later they were allowed to return to their homeland, only to find that encroachments by railroads and settlers with alcohol and diseases disturbed the peace and tranquility.

The Navajos have adapted again and again through the generations. They have found strength in the gradual evolution of traditional ceremonies to meet the challenges of a changing world. They are not a moribund culture, clinging to an impossible past, but a vibrant people utilizing ancient traditions to traverse new vistas successfully, adapting themselves so that however different and alien the world becomes they can continue in harmony and beauty.

Terry P. Wilson
Professor of Native American Studies
University of California, Berkeley

The Enchanted Land

The Navajo Nation is situated in the southwestern United States, with territories stretching from the northeast corner of Arizona into Utah and New Mexico, making it the largest reservation in the country by far. Additionally there are three noncontiguous smaller reservations under the tribal government.

Navajo country is one of the most spectacular landscapes of the United States; red sunburned arches, pinnacles, and mesas extend as far as the eye can see. When traveling through this magically

Previous page: The striking features of Monument Valley have inspired commentators to call it the eighth wonder of the world.

> "Although a sun-burnt desert of sand, sage brush, cactus, and piled-up debris of great volcanic eruptions, the Navajo country is a land of enchantment."
>
> —Joseph Campbell

sculpted land, one is transported to another planet. The magnificent Monument Valley has been called the eighth wonder of the world. The Navajo have made their home in this desert land as masters of their environment for centuries. An early traveler described the magical quality of a summer morning spent there:

"Slowly the darkness of early morn falls back before the shafts of a rising Sun. The keen arrows of light pierce its mantle, and it is driven fleeting to the west. The Sun is master; his morning rays dry the Earth. The vapor rises from the streams in the valley, at first in little threads of white, like smoke from a dying campfire; then gathering volume, it ascends until the course of the stream is

plainly marked by a pearly white drapery that curtains the brightness of the newborn day."

It is this rich texture of beauty in the midst of a stark and unforgiving landscape that both defines and shapes the Navajo way of life. To thrive in such a land is not easy, and requires an acutely developed awareness that life here is vulnerable to awesome powers beyond mere human control. The very way the Navajos speak of the passage of time reflects the mystery with which they endow the world around them. They measure time not in days but in nights—when darkness cloaks the features of the landscape in mystery, every sense is heightened, and each whisper of the wind, each call of a bird, is larger than life.

Perhaps the most striking element in the rich texture of Navajo spiritual and ceremonial life is its emphasis on beauty. Again and again in their chants and oral histories, the Navajos describe the harmony and rightness of things as "beautiful." Certainly their crafts, and the exquisite sand paintings that feature in so many of their ceremonials, reflect the Navajos' keenly developed aesthetic sensibilities.

The native inhabitants of this desert land call themselves Dineh, meaning "the people," and their cosmogony tells of four dark underworlds that had no Sun. They emerged from these worlds in order to find and settle this (the fifth) world of light, which they call the changeable world.

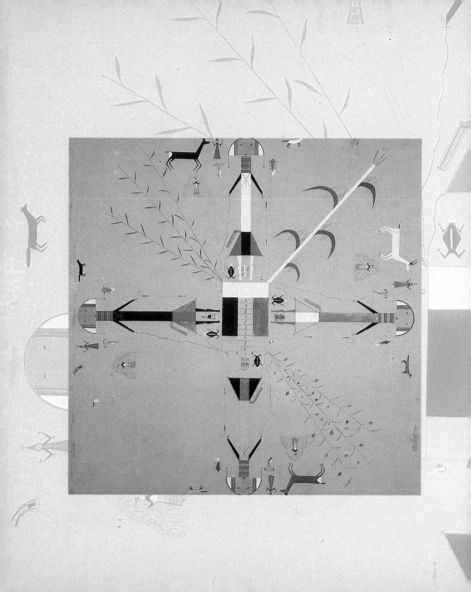

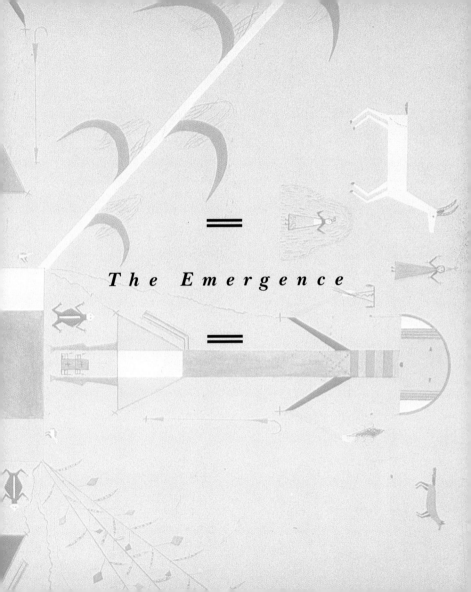

The Emergence

One of the many traditional Navajo accounts of their emergence begins by introducing all the inhabitants that had been brought to the fifth world. First Woman and First Man, with a multitude of other beings, emerged through a lake surrounded by four mountains located at the east, the south, the west, and the north. One of the first tasks of First Man was to build a home, and the symbology and songs derived from these accounts remain central to Navajo spiritual life today. The hogan is to the Navajo a microcosmic reflection of the larger universe, the dwelling-place of a life that is meant to be filled with happiness and end in a peaceful death of old age.

The First Hogan

In building the hogan, First Man created a cone-shaped structure using four main poles, each pole

Previous page: The wealth of symbols in this sand painting represents key elements of the Navajo accounts of the emergence. *Above:* Silver bracelet fashioned by a Navajo jeweler. *Opposite:* A hand-tinted postcard from 1909 shows a Navajo family outside their hogan.

representing one of the four directions. The east pole was a gift of the Earth, and that was where the door was placed, along with two marker stones set into the ground to symbolize that the hogan and the songs that accompanied its building would remain forever. The north pole was a gift from Mountain Woman, the west pole from Water Woman, and the south from Corn Woman. The activities of erecting each pole and covering the structure with sod were accompanied by songs that are still sung today as a hogan is built. A shortened version of this ceremonial is performed again whenever a hogan is consecrated for ceremonial uses.

The circular hogan of more recent times appears to be the result of

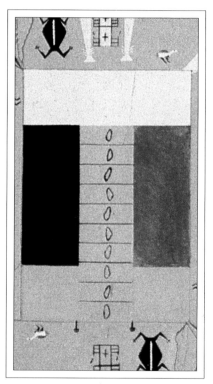

human ingenuity in the face of necessity. Back in the time of the emergence, when the conical hogan was not large enough to contain the gathering of all those who wanted to participate in a ceremony, the Holy People simply blew on it to make it bigger. Humans, however, had to devise another approach: they placed upright poles at each of the four points of the compass, and at the four points in between, linking them together with logs or branches and a circular roof. Thus the circumference of the hogan was not limited by the length of the poles available.

> **"It is my hogan where, from the doorway on and on, beauty radiates, it radiates from a woman, it increases its radius of beauty, golghane."**
>
> – *Slim Curly,*
> *Navajo Blessingway Singer*

The hogan, in addition to its function as a dwelling, is essential to all Navajo ceremonials. Therefore the larger, circular form of hogan is found today even in Navajo settlements which otherwise feature modern houses. Like the original conical hogan, the door of the circular hogan always faces east.

Opposite: The central feature of the sand painting on pages 18-19 shows the path used by the Navajos in reaching this world.

The Creation
of the
Sun and Moon

At the time of the emergence, after the first hogan was built, the Navajo tradition says, ". . . everyone rested. . . . The woman lay with her feet to the West, and the man lay with his feet to the East. Their heads crossed and their thoughts mingled, and these thoughts were sacred."

In understanding the Navajo world view one must take special note of the teachings that speak of the "inner forms" of things. These inner forms were set in place by First Man, First Woman, and their helpers soon after they emerged into the world. The concept of "inner form" might be described as being similar to the concept of a "spirit" or "soul" because without it, the Navajos say, the outer forms would be dead. But the Navajo concept does not carry with it the abstract, ethereal qualities normally associated with the words "spirit" and "soul." The inner forms are splendidly costumed, living entities in the Navajo tradition. The following account of the creation of the Sun and Moon gives a glimpse into the tangible beauty and reality of the "inner forms" as

it describes the actions of First Man and First Woman in creating the Sun and Moon:

First Woman and First Man whispered together during many nights. . . . They planned that there should be a sun, and day and night. . . . They spread a beautiful buckskin on the ground. This was the skin of a deer not killed by a weapon. On the buckskin they placed a perfect turquoise, round like the sun. It was as large as the height of an average man if he stretched his arm upward. They stood twelve tail feathers from the eagle around it, and also twelve tail feathers from the flicker. . . . After that they visited the different places where there was fire under the earth [and] found the Black Yei, who is

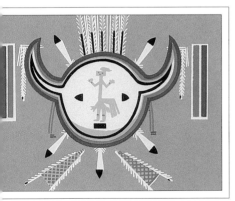

Previous page 24–25: A Blessingway sand painting depicting the Holy Mountains, the Sun and Moon, and other major elements of the Navajo universe. *Opposite:* This sand painting appears to have been specially created to depict both the Sun and Moon. Normally these two paintings would be created separately in a healing ceremonial. *Above:* A silver bow guard with a turquoise stone at the center.

also called the Fire God. He was asked to use fire to heat the great turquoise which they had planned to use as their sun.

They placed a perfect white shell on the buckskin below the turquoise that was to become the sun. This great, perfect, white shell was to become the moon. First Man planned to heat it with the first crystal that he had used for his fire. . . .

The Holy Ones asked the Turquoise Boy to enter the great, perfect turquoise that was to become the sun; and they asked the White Shell Girl to enter the great, perfect, white shell that was to become the moon. The Turquoise Boy was to carry a whistle made from the Male Reed. This whistle had twelve holes in it, and each time that the Turquoise Boy would blow on his whistle the earth would move one month in time. The White Shell Girl was also to carry a whistle. It was made from the Female Reed, and with it she should move the tides of the sea.

Above: Painting of a fire dance ceremony by contemporary Navajo artist Beatien Yazz. *Right:* Brilliant colors and patterns distinguish the blankets and rugs created by Navajo weavers.

As with most Native American cultures, the Navajo universe found within these origin accounts is an all-inclusive unity viewed as an orderly system of interrelated elements. Almost from the beginning, First Man and First Woman and other holy beings set in place the "inner forms" of natural phenomena. Their thoughts and actions are sacred in the sense that it is they who decide how the world should and will work, and their inherent divine wisdom is both proved and framed for all time in the different oral traditions, from the emergence to the building of the first hogan and the creation of Sun and Moon. In this divine "making," First Man and First Woman and the holy beings create the present world, the Navajo universe.

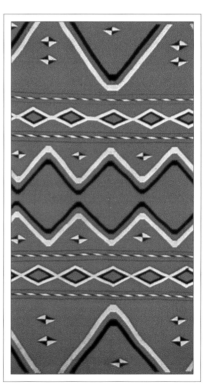

The Four Holy Mountains

Once the people had settled in the fifth world, they established the boundaries of their territories. Jeff King, a Navajo singer who gave the following account in the 1940s, used the present-day names of the four mountains, but of course the Navajos had their own names for these sacred places. Mount Taylor, for example, was called "Tongue Mountain," and the mountain now called San Francisco Peak was known as "Light Shines from It."

When the people were ready and had everything to dress the mountains in, they stood on a rainbow and traveled to the east, to plant the Holy Mountain of the East. They put down a blanket of white shell and on it some sand of the mountains of the world below. They wrapped this up in

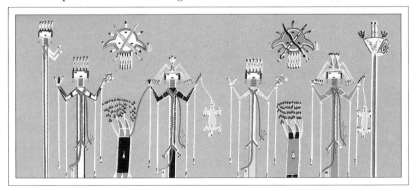

its blanket, and they planted it to the east. And since they all agreed and they all wanted it, it became and was called Blanca Peak. With the Mountain of the South they did likewise, only it was planted on a turquoise blanket and was made of sand and turquoise, and it was called Mount Taylor. The Mountain of the West was made on an abalone blanket and out of sand and abalone, and it was called San Francisco Peak. The Mountain of the North was made on a jet blanket and was made of jet and sand, and it was called La

"Facing this way from the summit of Blanca Peak the two [First Man and First Woman] sat down side by side. As they viewed the scene below they found it extremely beautiful...beauty radiated from it everywhere."

—Jeff King

Plata Range. . . . After these mountains had been made, the people decided to place a holy person in each, to guard it and to listen to the prayers, songs, and offerings made to it. . . . In the Mountain of the East they put Talking God of the East; in the Mountain of the South, Call God of the South; in the Mountain of the West, Talking God of the West; in the Mountain of the North, Call God of the North.

Far left: The four Mountain Gods as depicted in a Beautyway sand painting.
Left: Hand-crafted Navajo doll.

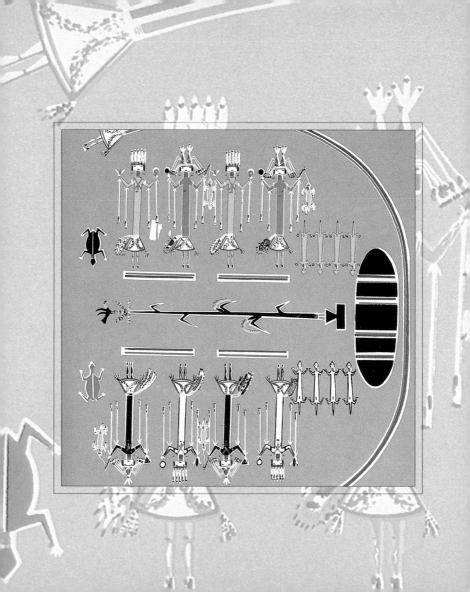

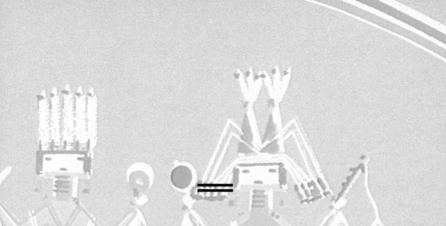

Navajo Ceremonial Traditions

There are no organized priesthoods or fixed places of worship in the Navajo spiritual tradition. Neither is there a ceremonial calendar, though there are some traditional dates when ceremonials may be conducted for the benefit of the whole tribe. The Navajo's relationship with the world of spirit is an individual one, and it is when a person is out of harmony with this world that sickness or misfortune can ensue.

> "The mountains, I become part of it. . .
> The herbs, the evergreen,
> I become part of it.
> The morning mists, the clouds, the gathering waters,
> I become part of it.
> The dew drops, the pollen, I become part of it."
>
> *Navajo Beautyway Chant*

Ceremonials are performed by singers, or "medicine men," whenever an individual needs them. For example, when a Navajo is troubled by bad dreams, sickness, insecurity, fear, or some other affliction, the first step is to determine which action has brought about the disharmony. Generally, this is achieved by discussion between the afflicted person and his or her relatives. Sometimes a diagnosis might be needed by a practitioner of Handtremblingway, a

Previous page: The Weasel People portrayed here gave the Navajos the medicine pouches used in healing ceremonials.
Opposite: Detail of a Navajo blanket.

N,
La Plata Range
Call God
Jet

N,
San Francisco Pk.
Talking God
Abalone

E.
Blanca Pk.
Talking God
White Shell

S.
Mt. Taylor
Call God
Turquoise

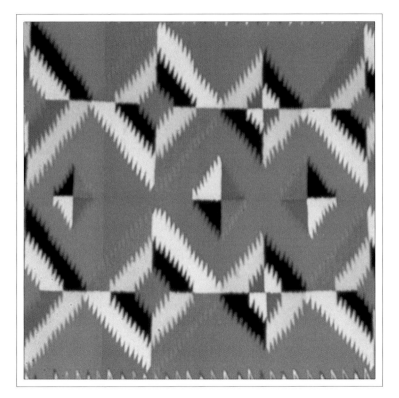

traditional divining method used to determine the cause of disease. Once the cause is determined, the next step is to call on a singer who specializes in treating this particular condition so that he can set things right again. If there is any doubt, parts of two or three ceremonials might be used experimentally to determine which seems to bring about the desired result.

The all-encompassing Navajo universe contains both good and evil, and the forces that determine the interactions within this universe are both benevolent and dangerous. Natural phenomena, such as lightning, thunder, and wind, and also animals, such as bears, snakes, frogs and coyotes, can be dangerous if an individual has behaved improperly toward them. Supernatural forces such as ghosts and witches can cause harm, and ceremonial objects may be touched at improper times, or even with an improper attitude, and thereby cause disease. Such disease may be dispelled with

Above: Silver box inset with turquoise stones, created by a Navajo jeweler.

the performance of ceremonies and prayers that restore harmony or bring danger under control.

These ceremonies and prayers are not intended to glorify or thank the holy beings of the Navajo pantheon, but rather to invoke their power to help the essence of the sick individual return to harmony. In large part the ceremonies take the form of chants, and all these chants or songs have been given to the Navajos by representatives of the spirit world.

The ceremonials used in restoring balance and harmony according to the Navajo teachings are known as Chantways. There are several Chantways, and each Chantway has subgroups according to the disharmonies and imbalances they are intended to cure. The Navajo ceremonial complex is derived from an extensive interlocking web of ancient traditions that can only be referred to here, but the list of Chantways (on page 42) gives a sense of their complexity and depth.

It should be understood that the specific causes of disease or disharmony are not necessarily meant to be taken literally---a Red Antway chant, for example, is not necessarily applied only to heal a person who suffers from a direct contact with these ants.

The true significance of each of the different Chantways, and the determining factor in choosing a particular Chantway to heal a disease, lies in the qualities of the inner forms, or powers, of the phenomena or creatures associated with them. The afflicted person's suffering has been brought about by improper interaction with one of these powers, but this does not always imply a direct encounter with the outer form of the given animal or phenomenon.

In the Navajo healing system, the process of diagnosis and treatment is intimately woven into the entire spiritual tradition, with all its characters playing their unique roles and contributing their special gifts toward the restoration of the balance and beauty of the universe.

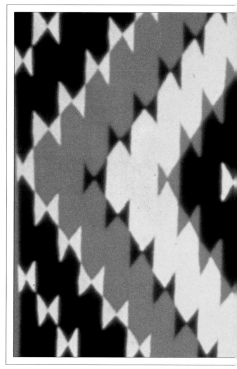

Right: Wool blanket created by Navajo weaver.

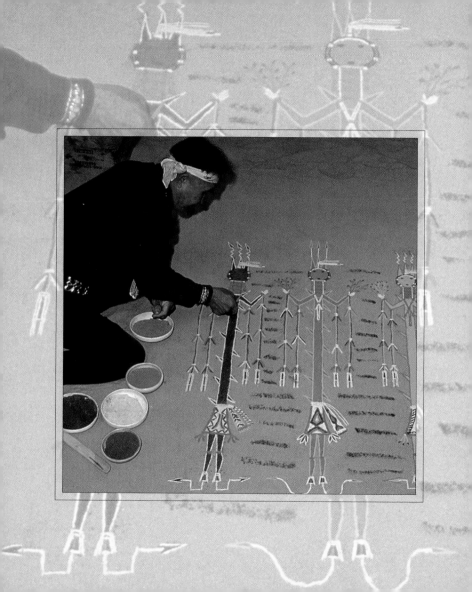

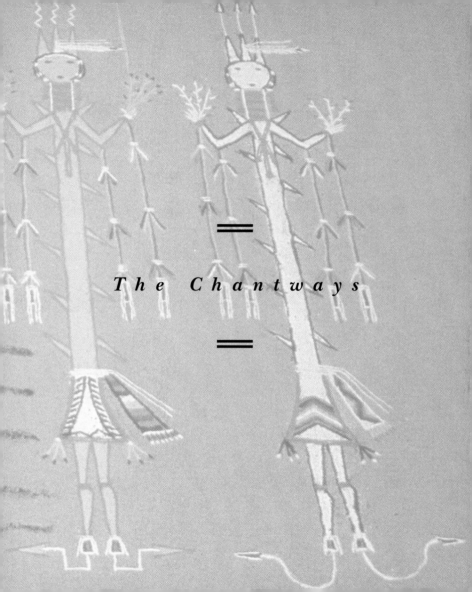

The Chantways

SHOOTINGWAY
...lightning, snakes, arrows

RED ANTWAY
...infections from ants or horned toads

BIG STARWAY
...water or frost

MOUNTAINWAY
...bears, porcupines, weasels

BEAUTYWAY
...snakes

NIGHTWAY
...supernaturals

BIG GODWAY
...deer or other game

PLUMEWAY
...sexual excess or incest

COYOTEWAY
...coyotes

WINDWAY
...winds, snakes, cactus, clouds, sun, moon

GHOSTWAY
...sickness caused by witches or ghosts

ENEMYWAY
...ancient war ceremonial for protection and purification of warriors; now used to cure sicknesses believed to be caused by ghosts of non-Navajos.

LIFEWAY
...accidents

HANDTREMBLINGWAY
...Used for divining the nature of illness and determining what cure should be applied

Many ancient chant complexes have today become obsolete, as a result of the changing circumstances of Navajo life. The singers, or medicine men, learn from oral tradition and usually specialize in a few chants, although they might know parts of several more. The ceremonials may be performed over a period of two, three, five, or nine nights.

The singer is approached by the relatives and friends of the sick person, and the payment for the ceremony is always arranged in advance, the price depending on the gravity of the illness and the consequent length of the ceremony (a very sick person might need a nine-day chant).

Blessingway

Every healing ceremonial begins with the consecration of the hogan by the singer. These consecration rites are part of the Blessingway ceremonials, which have been described as the "spinal column" of the songs and chants of all the other Navajo Chantways. The Blessingway rites alone are not used specifically in healing. However, they are an essential component of all healing rituals.

Father Berard Haile, who lived with the Navajos and meticulously recorded their ceremonials in the early twentieth century, has described the role of Blessingway as follows: "At the end of every

Previous pages 40–41: Navajo John Burnside demonstrates sand painting techniques at a crafts exhibition in Arizona.

performance of a chant, the singer lays aside his rattle and sings at least one Blessingway song to justify the chant, to insure its effectiveness, to correct inadvertent omission of essential song and prayer words, to correct errors in sand paintings and in cutting prayersticks."

People] in colors."

There are a limited number of drypaintings that are exclusive to Blessingway. These are generally painted not with sand as a base, but only with the materials used for pigmentation in sand paintings, such as pollens, dried flowers, and cornmeal.

Blessingway lays the foundation for the whole system of Chantways, including the various elements of the sand paintings. Again to quote Father Haile, "Blessingway paints a word picture, while the sand paintings of the other Chantways depict these garments [of the Holy

Blessingway songs always mark the beginning and end of all the other Chantway ceremonials. In addition, there are several Blessingway ceremonials performed in circumstances where peace, harmony, and good fortune are desired. For example, Blessingway ceremonies are performed to celebrate birth, adolescence, and marriage, to consecrate a new home or important possessions, or as part of the installation of a new tribal official.

Most Navajo families have such a Mountain Soil Bundle that is passed on from one generation to the next, and is counted among a family's most precious possessions.

Only one ritual object is absolutely required for a Blessingway rite, and that is a Mountain Soil Bundle. This small bundle consists of soils gathered from each of the holy mountains, wrapped in a buckskin that is tied and decorated with stones according to tradition.

The Healing Ceremonials

The first step in any healing ceremonial is to consecrate the hogan of the person to be healed, as the rites must be performed on sacred ground for the cure to be effective. As part of this consecration ceremony, the singer sprinkles

Opposite: Silver squash-blossom necklace with pale turquoise pendant feature. *Above:* Detail of blanket worn by a Navajo chief in the late 19th century. *Following page 47:* Traditional silver and turquoise ornamentation on belt made by Navajo craftsman.

cornmeal on the four directional posts or roof beams of the hogan. After sunset on the first day, a special "unraveling ceremony" is performed to dispel evil forces. A bundle of herbs or feathers is placed on the body of the patient, tied in such a way that the bundle will unravel when the string is pulled at the appropriate time during the chanting.

In the morning, especially during the longer ceremonials, a sweat and emetic ceremony may be prepared, to purify the patient and any others who are participating in the cure.

"It is surprising, surprising...yi ye! It is the very inner form of Earth that continues to move with me, that has risen with me, that indeed remains stationary with me. Now it is the inner form of long life, of happiness... It is surprising, surprising!"

- Slim Curly, Navajo Blessingway Singer

These are just a few elements of many that make up a healing ceremonial —there are other rites involving prayer offerings to attract the Holy People, the placement of prayer sticks in preparation for the sand paintings, and ceremonies to further prepare the patient for healing.

The Chantway employed in each particular case determines the procedures to be followed in the ceremonial, and the narrative accompanying the rites puts each element into context. The ceremonial usually begins with an explanation by the singer of the origin tradition belonging to the Chantway to be used. He might start with an account from the time of the emergence, and this explanation is given well before the start of the specific rituals of the ceremonial. This narrative establishes a foundation for the chant to follow, and notifies the appropriate powers that their help is requested in curing the patient.

As the Chantway proceeds, these helping powers are introduced through the narrative itself. Thus the patient hears of their adventures, takes heed of the lessons implied in them, and is reunited with his or her own innate capacity for harmonious interaction within the framework of the Navajo universe.

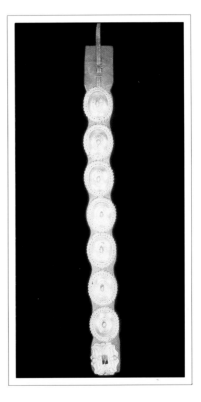

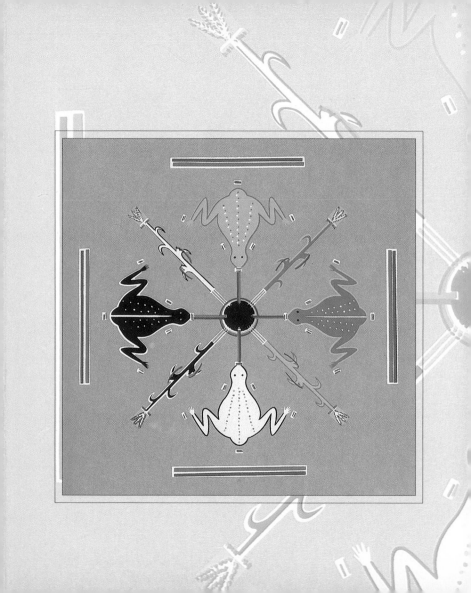

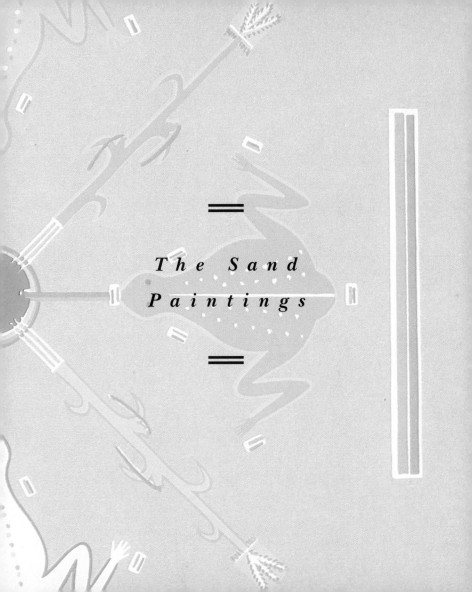

The Sand Paintings

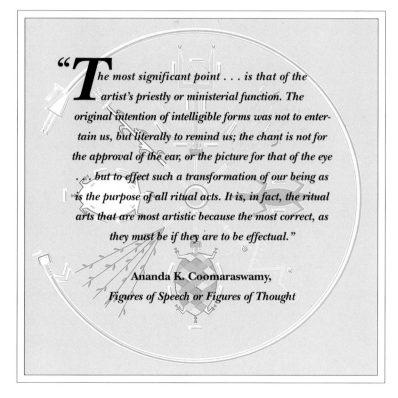

"*The most significant point . . . is that of the artist's priestly or ministerial function. The original intention of intelligible forms was not to entertain us, but literally to remind us; the chant is not for the approval of the ear, or the picture for that of the eye . . . but to effect such a transformation of our being as is the purpose of all ritual acts. It is, in fact, the ritual arts that are most artistic because the most correct, as they must be if they are to be effectual.*"

Ananda K. Coomaraswamy,
Figures of Speech or Figures of Thought

The creation and use of sand paintings in Navajo healing rites generally occur on the last day of a ceremonial. By this time, all the other component rites of the ceremonial have been performed at least two or three times, so the patient is well prepared for this important part of the healing process.

The paintings themselves portray the entities who have been chosen to assist in the patient's cure. In a sense these entities have been "trapped" within the drawings. The singer's retelling of a traditional incident in song and chant has by now brought the patient to a point where he or she can readily understand and identify with the forms depicted in the painting. This understanding and identification serve to make the patient powerful, strong, and immune to sickness, as are the pictured entities.

Once the sand painting is complete, the patient is often directed to literally sit or lie down within it. Alternatively, the colored sands may be applied to the sick person's body. Through participating in this ritual, the patient is taken away from the present reality of his illness and is allowed

Previous pages 48–49: Sand painting used in healing ceremonies to cure diseases caused by improper contact with the powers of the frog. *Opposite background and following pages 52-53:* Details from a sand painting used to treat those harmed by lightning, water, or in a corn, bean, squash, or tobacco field.

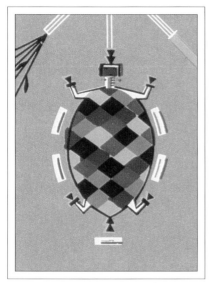

ceremony. In a sense, the stronger the identification with the powers portrayed in the painting, the more effective the cure.

The sand paintings are healing by virtue of their ability both to draw out evil from the body and to provide healing power. After the ceremony the painting is erased and the sands put away in a place where whatever evil has been absorbed by them can do no harm.

entrance to the spirit world. There he or she also becomes a spirit for the duration of the ritual, returning to his or her earthly form only at the end of the

The sand is colored according to tradition with a variety of natural pigments: cornmeals, pollens, pulverized flower petals, and charcoal. The "painting" is achieved by allowing the sand mixture to trickle between thumb and flexed index finger in a neat line. These paintings are not necessarily created by the singer or medicine man himself, but are always directed by him in every detail. This gives apprentices the opportunity to learn the different designs pertaining to each ceremonial through practice.

When the Holy People gave the Navajo instructions in the use of the sand paintings, they strictly prohibited the reproduction of these paintings in permanent form. In following this directive the Navajos have forbidden photography of the paintings and only a few watercolor and crayon reproductions exist. There are paintings of

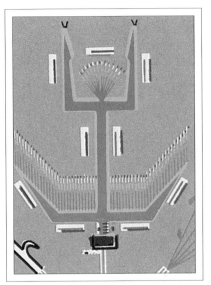

sand glued to backings that are made and sold to non-Navajos, but these are purposely flawed so that the ancient restrictions are not violated.

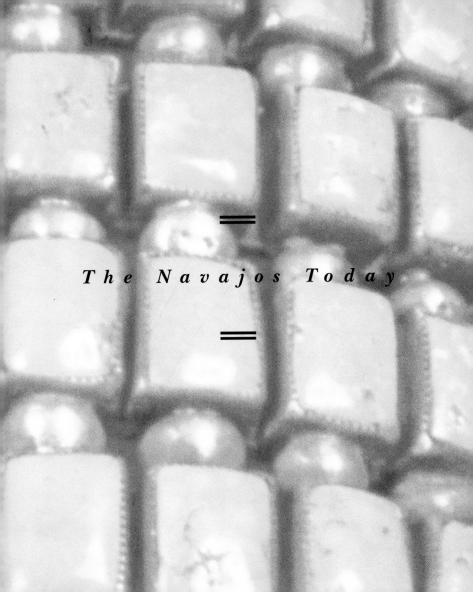

The Navajos Today

From their earlier times as tribal groups of nomadic and restless warriors, the Navajos have become a peace-loving people. Everyday life revolves around the activities of agriculture and the raising of horses and cattle, along with a thriving industry in the breeding of sheep and goats. They are also known as skilled jewelers, and make some of the most beautiful handwoven blankets of any of the Native American people.

The outer forms of Navajo life today are the result of each generation's adaptation to the changing circumstances of their times. Undoubtedly these resourceful people will continue to adapt the outer forms of their lives in response to the changing circumstances faced by generations to come. But the teachings and traditions that have remained constant in the lives of those who walk in beauty, the inner forms that direct and enrich their ceremonials, will certainly endure. They are renewed in all their splendor each time the Navajos gather together to sing and chant their ancient tribute to the beauty of the universe.

Previous pages 54–55: The pattern of turquoise stones on this bracelet suggests the corn that is a staple food of the Navajos. *Opposite background and following page 58:* Detail of one of the blankets for which the Navajos are famous.

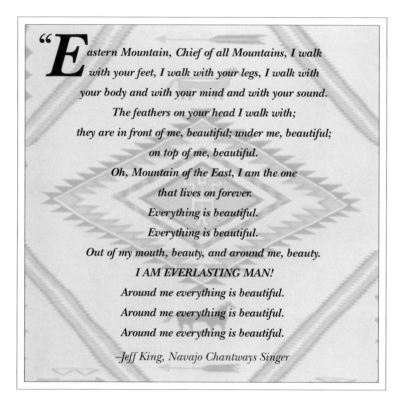

"*Eastern Mountain, Chief of all Mountains, I walk
with your feet, I walk with your legs, I walk with
your body and with your mind and with your sound.
The feathers on your head I walk with;
they are in front of me, beautiful; under me, beautiful;
on top of me, beautiful.
Oh, Mountain of the East, I am the one
that lives on forever.
Everything is beautiful.
Everything is beautiful.
Out of my mouth, beauty, and around me, beauty.
I AM EVERLASTING MAN!
Around me everything is beautiful.
Around me everything is beautiful.
Around me everything is beautiful.*

—Jeff King, Navajo Chantways Singer

BIBLIOGRAPHY

Campbell, Joseph. *The Way of the Animal Powers—Historical Atlas of World Mythology.* Times Books, London, 1984.

Coomaraswamy, Ananda K. *Figures of Speech or Figures of Thought,* Luzac & Co., London, 1946.

Lipps, Oscar H. *A Little History of the Navajos.* The Torch Press, Cedar Rapids, Iowa, 1909, and Avanyu Publishing, Inc, Albuquerque, New Mexico, 1989

Oakes, Maud; Joseph Campbell, and Jeff King. *Where the Two Came to Their Father: A Navajo War Ceremonial. Given by Jeff King, text and paintings recorded by Oakes, edited and with commentary by Campbell. (Bollingen Series I)* Pantheon Books, New York, 1943; 2nd edition, Princeton University Press, Princeton, 1969.

O'Bryan, Aileen. "The Dîné: Origin Myths of the Navaho Indians." *Bureau of American Ethonology, Bulletin 163.* Washington D.C., 1956.

Reichard, Gladys A. *Navaho Religion: A Study of Symbolism. (Bollingen Series XVIII)* Pantheon Books, New York, 1950.

Wyman, Leland C., *Beautyway: A Navaho Ceremonial. (Bollingen Series LIII)* Pantheon Books, New York, 1957; 2nd edition, Princeton University Press, Princeton, 1985.

Wyman, Leland C. *(Ed.), Blessingway, with Three Versions of the Myth Recorded and Translated from the Navaho by Father Berard Haile.* University of Arizona Press, Tucson, Arizona, 1970.

Brady, Margaret K. *"Some Kind of Power": Navajo Children's Skinwalker Narratives.* University of Utah Press, Salt Lake City, Utah, 1984.

Bingham, Sam and Janet Bingham, *eds. Between Sacred Mountains: Navajo Stories and Lessons from the Land. (Sun Tracks)* University of Arizona Press, Tucson, Arizona, 1982.

Brugge, David M. And Charlotte J. Frisbie, *eds. Navajo Religion and Culture: Selected Views.* Museum of New Mexico Press, Santa Fe, New Mexico, 1982.

Haile, Father Berard. *Navajo Coyote Tales: The Curly to Aheedlinii Version.* University of Nebraska Press, Lincoln, Nebraska, 1984.

Kluckhohn, Clyde and Dorothea C. Leighton. *The Navajo.* Harvard University Press, Cambridge, Mass., 1946.

Rapoport, Robert N. *Changing Navaho Religious Values. Papers of the Peabody Museum of American Archaeology and Ethnology, Vol. 42, No. 2.* Cambridge, Mass., 1954.

Zolbrod, Paul. *Dini Bahani: The Navajo Creation Story.* University of New Mexico Press, Albuquerque, New Mexico, 1984.

ACKNOWLEDGMENTS

Every effort has been made to trace all present copyright holders of the material used in this book, whether companies or individuals. Any omission is unintentional and we will be pleased to correct errors in future editions of this book.

Text acknowledgments:

p. 50: From *Figures of Speech or Figures of Thought,* by Ananda K. Coomaraswamy, Luzac & Co., London, 1946.

pp. 30-31, 57: From *Where the Two Came to Their Father: A Navajo War Ceremonial,* given by Jeff King, text and paintings recorded by Maud Oakes, edited and with commentary by Joseph Campbell, (Bollingen Series I), Pantheon Books, New York, 1943; 2nd edition, Princeton University Press, Princeton, 1969. Reproduced by permission of Princeton University Press.

pp. 16-17, back cover: From Oscar H. Lipps, *A Little History of the Navajos,* The Torch Press, Cedar Rapids, Iowa, 1909, and Avanyu Publishing, Inc., Albuquerque, New Mexico, 1989. Reproduced by permission of Avanyu Publishing.

pp. 27-28: From Aileen O'Bryan, "The Dîné: Origin Myths of the Navaho Indians," in *Bureau of American Ethnology,*

Bulletin 163, Washington D.C., 1956. Courtesy Smithsonian Institution Press.

pp. 23, 31, 43-44, 46: Reprinted from *Blessingway,* by Leland C. Wyman by permission of the University of Arizona Press, Albuquerque, New Mexico, Copyright (c) 1970.

Special thanks go to Terry P. Wilson, Professor of Native American Studies at the University of California, Berkeley. His help in checking the accuracy of information and the sensitivity of the language used in this work has been invaluable.

Picture acknowledgments:

Reproduced by permission of the Museum of Northern Arizona; Pages: 8, 14, 40.
Reproduced by permission of the National Museum of The American Indian, Smithsonian Institution; Pages: 7, 10, 20, 27, 28, 29, 31, 35, 36, 38, 44, 45, 47, 54, 57, 58, cover.
Peter Newark's Western Americana; Pages: 12, 13, 21.
Reproduced by permission of the Bollingen Foundation, Princeton University; Pages: 4, 24, 26, 30, 32, 48, 50, 52, 53.
By permission of the museum of Navaho Ceremonial Art, Santa Fe; Pages: 18, 22.